How to Add Another Zero to Your Business Sales in 2024-25

Introduction

Importance of Scaling Business Sales:

Scaling business sales is a transformative goal that can significantly impact your company's growth, profitability, and market presence.

Adding another zero to your sales figures means exponentially increasing your revenue, which can open doors to new opportunities, enable greater investment in innovation, and strengthen your competitive position.

The process of scaling requires a strategic approach that involves understanding your market, refining your product offerings, optimizing your sales and marketing efforts, leveraging technology, and expanding into new markets.

For businesses, particularly those in competitive industries, achieving significant sales growth is crucial.

It not only enhances financial stability but also provides the resources needed to invest in research and development, improve operational efficiencies, and attract top talent.

Moreover, a substantial increase in sales can enhance your brand's reputation, making it easier to secure partnerships, funding, and market share.

Overview of Strategies to Be Discussed

Achieving exponential sales growth involves a multifaceted strategy. These suggestions will cover the following key areas:

1. Market Analysis and Understanding Your Customer:

Conducting thorough market research, identifying target demographics, understanding customer needs and pain points, and using customer feedback to drive improvements.

2. Enhancing Product/Service Offerings:

Innovating existing products/services, expanding product lines, improving quality and value, and adapting to market trends and customer demands.

3. Optimizing Sales and Marketing Strategies:

Building a robust marketing plan, leveraging digital and traditional marketing methods, personalizing marketing efforts, enhancing your brand's online presence, and implementing data-driven marketing techniques.

4. Boosting Online Sales Channels:

Improving e-commerce platforms, utilizing marketplaces, enhancing website UX/UI, optimizing for mobile sales, and leveraging affiliate marketing and partnerships.

5. Improving Sales Processes and Techniques:

Streamlining sales processes, training and empowering your sales team, using CRM tools effectively, implementing effective sales techniques, and building a customer-focused sales approach.

6. Leveraging Technology and Automation:

Implementing AI and machine learning in sales, using automation tools for marketing and sales, adopting new technologies to streamline operations, and leveraging data analytics and big data.

7. Expanding into New Markets:

Identifying potential new markets, strategies for market entry, localizing your approach for different regions, and overcoming challenges in new market expansion.

8. Building Strategic Partnerships and Alliances:

Identifying potential partners, building mutually beneficial relationships, leveraging partnerships for growth, and case studies of successful partnerships.

9. Financial Management and Investment for Growth:

Managing cash flow for scalability, investing in growth opportunities, securing funding and financing options, and cost management and optimization.

10. Monitoring Progress and Adjusting Strategies:

Setting key performance indicators (KPIs), regularly reviewing and analyzing performance, being flexible and adjusting strategies as needed.

Setting Realistic Goals and Expectations

While aiming to add another zero to your business sales is an ambitious and exciting goal, it is crucial to set realistic expectations and milestones.

Growth does not happen overnight; it requires consistent effort, strategic planning, and adaptability.

Setting achievable targets helps in maintaining motivation and focus while allowing you to measure progress and make necessary adjustments.

Realistic goals should be specific, measurable, attainable, relevant, and time-bound (SMART).

For instance, instead of setting a vague goal like "increase sales," aim for "increase sales by 50% in the next 12 months."

Break down this overarching goal into smaller, actionable steps, such as enhancing your marketing efforts, expanding your product line, or entering new markets.

Regularly monitoring your progress through key performance indicators (KPIs) and being prepared to adjust your strategies based on performance and market feedback is essential.

Flexibility and responsiveness to changing market conditions will help ensure sustained growth and long-term success.

Market Analysis and Understanding Your Customer

Conducting Thorough Market Research

Market research forms the backbone of any successful sales strategy.

Understanding the dynamics of your market allows you to identify growth opportunities, understand customer needs, and stay ahead of competitors. Here are key steps to conducting effective market research:

- Identify Market Trends:

Staying updated with the latest trends in your industry is crucial.

Use market reports, industry publications, and online resources to gather information on emerging trends, consumer behavior, and the competitive landscape.

Tools like Google Trends, industry-specific studies, and market analysis platforms can provide valuable insights.

- **Analyze Competitors:**

A detailed analysis of your competitors helps you understand their strengths and weaknesses.

Identify their product offerings, pricing strategies, marketing tactics, and customer reviews.

This analysis can help you find gaps in the market that your business can exploit.

- Survey Your Customers:

 Direct feedback from your customers is invaluable. Use surveys, interviews, and focus groups to gather insights into their preferences, pain points, and expectations.

 This information can guide your product development and marketing strategies. Tools like SurveyMonkey, Google Forms, and Typeform can facilitate this process.

Identifying Target Demographics

Knowing who your customers are is essential for creating targeted marketing campaigns and product offerings.

Here's how to identify and segment your target demographics:

- **Demographic Segmentation:**

 Break down your customer base into categories such as age, gender, income level, education, and occupation.

 This helps you understand the specific needs and preferences of different segments.

 Use data analytics tools like Google Analytics, customer relationship management (CRM) systems, and market research reports to gather demographic information.

- **Psychographic Segmentation:**

 Go beyond demographics and consider the psychological aspects of your customers, such as their values, attitudes, interests, and lifestyles.

 This deeper understanding can help you create more personalized and compelling marketing messages. Psychographic data can be collected through surveys, social media insights, and customer feedback.

- **Behavioral Segmentation:**

 Analyze the purchasing behavior of your customers, including their buying frequency, brand loyalty, and spending habits.

 This information can help you identify high-value customers and tailor your marketing efforts accordingly.

 Behavioral data can be obtained from your CRM system, e-commerce platform, and analytics tools.

Understanding Customer Needs and Pain Points

To effectively meet the needs of your customers, you must understand their pain points and challenges.

Here are some ways to gain these insights:

- **Customer Feedback:**

 Regularly collect and analyze customer feedback through surveys, reviews, and direct interactions.

 Pay attention to recurring issues and complaints, as they can highlight areas for improvement.

 Tools like Zendesk, Trustpilot, and Google Reviews can help you gather and analyze customer feedback.

- Social Media Monitoring:

Monitor social media platforms for mentions of your brand and industry.

Social listening tools like Hootsuite, Sprout Social, and Brandwatch can help you track conversations and identify common themes and concerns among your audience.

- **Competitive Analysis:**

 Look at the feedback and reviews of your competitors.

 This can provide insights into what customers like and dislike about similar products or services, helping you improve your offerings.

 Tools like SimilarWeb, SEMrush, and Ahrefs can assist in competitive analysis.

Using Customer Feedback to Drive Improvements

Customer feedback is a valuable resource for driving continuous improvement in your business.

Here's how to leverage it effectively:

- **Implement Changes Based on Feedback:**

  Take customer feedback seriously and make necessary changes to your products, services, or processes.

  This shows customers that you value their opinions and are committed to meeting their needs.

  Use project management tools like Asana, Trello, and Monday.com to track and implement changes.

- **Communicate Improvements:**

　Inform your customers about the changes you've made based on their feedback.

　This can enhance customer loyalty and trust, as they see that their input directly impacts your business.

　Use email marketing tools like Mailchimp, Constant Contact, and Sendinblue to communicate improvements.

- **Measure Impact:**

 Track the impact of the changes you've implemented.

 Use metrics such as customer satisfaction scores, repeat purchase rates, and sales growth to evaluate the effectiveness of your improvements.

 Analytics tools like Google Analytics, Mixpanel, and Pendo can help measure the impact.

Enhancing Product/Service Offerings

Innovating Existing Products/Services

Innovation is key to staying competitive and meeting the evolving needs of your customers.

Here are some strategies to innovate your existing products or services:

- **Customer-Centric Innovation:**

 Focus on creating products or services that address the specific needs and pain points of your customers.

 Use customer feedback and market research to guide your innovation efforts.

 Implement regular brainstorming sessions and innovation workshops to generate new ideas.

- Incorporate New Technologies:

Leverage new technologies to enhance your products or services.

This could include integrating AI, IoT, or blockchain technology, depending on your industry.

Stay updated with the latest technological advancements and consider how they can be applied to your offerings.

- Continuous Improvement:

Adopt a mindset of continuous improvement.

Regularly update and refine your products or services based on customer feedback and market trends.

Use agile methodologies and iterative processes to accelerate innovation cycles.

Expanding Product Lines

Expanding your product lines can help you reach new customers and increase sales.

Here are some approaches to consider:

- Product Line Extensions:

Introduce new variations of your existing products, such as different sizes, colors, or features.

This can appeal to different segments of your market and increase your overall sales.

Conduct market research and gather customer feedback to identify potential extensions.

- **Diversification:**

Develop new products that are related to your existing offerings but cater to different customer needs.

This can help you tap into new markets and reduce reliance on a single product.

Use tools like SWOT analysis and Ansoff Matrix to evaluate diversification opportunities.

- Collaborations and Partnerships:

Partner with other companies to co-develop new products.

This can bring in new expertise, resources, and customer bases, accelerating your product development efforts.

Look for complementary businesses and explore joint venture opportunities.

Improving Quality and Value

Quality and value are crucial factors that influence customer satisfaction and loyalty.

Here are some ways to enhance the quality and value of your products or services:

- Focus on Quality Control:

Implement rigorous quality control processes to ensure that your products or services consistently meet high standards.

This can help reduce defects, returns, and customer complaints.

Use tools like Six Sigma, Lean, and Total Quality Management (TQM) to improve quality control.

- Add Value-Added Features:

Enhance your products or services with additional features or benefits that provide extra value to your customers.

This could include extended warranties, free shipping, or exclusive content.

Conduct competitor analysis and customer surveys to identify potential value-added features.

- **Competitive Pricing:**

 Ensure that your pricing is competitive and reflects the value that your products or services offer.

 Conduct regular pricing analyses to stay in line with market trends and customer expectations.

 Use pricing strategies like cost-plus pricing, value-based pricing, and dynamic pricing to optimize your pricing.

Adapting to Market Trends and Customer Demands

Staying adaptable and responsive to market trends and customer demands is essential for sustained growth.

Here are some strategies to help you stay ahead of the curve:

- **Monitor Industry Trends:**

Keep a close eye on industry trends and emerging technologies.

Attend industry conferences, read relevant publications, and network with other professionals to stay informed.

Use trend analysis tools like TrendWatching, Mintel, and Gartner to identify key trends.

- Flexible Product Development:

Adopt a flexible approach to product development that allows you to quickly pivot and adapt to changing market conditions.

Use agile methodologies like Scrum and Kanban to accelerate innovation cycles.

- Customer-Centric Approach:

Continuously engage with your customers to understand their evolving needs and preferences.

Use this information to guide your product development and marketing strategies.

Implement customer advisory boards and user testing to gather feedback and insights.

Optimizing Sales and Marketing Strategies

Building a Robust Marketing Plan

A comprehensive marketing plan is essential for driving sales and achieving your growth objectives.

Here are the key components of an effective marketing plan:

- Market Research and Analysis:

Conduct thorough market research to understand your target audience, competitors, and industry trends.

Use this information to identify opportunities and set realistic marketing goals.

Tools like SWOT analysis, PEST analysis, and Porter's Five Forces can help in market analysis.

- **Marketing Objectives and Goals:**

Define clear, measurable marketing objectives and goals that align with your overall business strategy.

These could include increasing brand awareness, generating leads, or boosting sales.

Use the SMART criteria (Specific, Measurable, Achievable, Relevant, Time-bound) to set your goals.

- **Marketing Strategies and Tactics:**

Develop detailed strategies and tactics for achieving your marketing objectives.

This could include content marketing, social media marketing, email marketing, search engine optimization (SEO), and paid advertising.

Create a marketing calendar to plan and schedule your activities.

- Budget and Resources:

Allocate a budget for your marketing activities and ensure you have the necessary resources, including personnel and tools, to execute your plan effectively.

Use budgeting tools like PlanGuru, LivePlan, and QuickBooks to manage your marketing budget.

- **Performance Metrics and Evaluation:**

 Define key performance indicators (KPIs) to measure the success of your marketing efforts.

 Regularly review and analyze your performance to identify areas for improvement.

 Use analytics tools like Google Analytics, HubSpot, and Marketo to track and measure your marketing performance.

Leveraging Digital Marketing

Digital marketing offers numerous opportunities to reach a wider audience and drive sales.

Here are some key digital marketing strategies to consider:

- Search Engine Optimization (SEO):

Optimize your website and content for search engines to increase organic traffic.

Focus on keyword research, on-page optimization, and building high-quality backlinks.

Use SEO tools like Ahrefs, SEMrush, and Moz to improve your SEO efforts.

- **Content Marketing:**

 Create valuable, informative, and engaging content that addresses the needs and interests of your target audience.

 Use blogs, videos, infographics, and social media posts to distribute your content.

 Use content marketing tools like HubSpot, Contentful, and CoSchedule to manage your content strategy.

- Social Media Marketing:

Leverage social media platforms to connect with your audience, build brand awareness, and drive traffic to your website.

Use a mix of organic and paid strategies to maximize your reach.

Use social media management tools like Hootsuite, Buffer, and Sprout Social to manage your social media campaigns.

- **Email Marketing:**

 Develop targeted email campaigns to nurture leads and retain existing customers.

 Use personalized and relevant content to engage your subscribers and encourage conversions.

 Use email marketing tools like Mailchimp, Constant Contact, and Sendinblue to create and manage your email campaigns.

- **Pay-Per-Click (PPC) Advertising:**

 Use PPC advertising to drive targeted traffic to your website.

 Platforms like Google Ads and social media ads allow you to reach potential customers based on their interests and search behavior.

 Use PPC tools like Google Ads, Facebook Ads Manager, and WordStream to manage your PPC campaigns.

Utilizing Traditional Marketing Methods

While digital marketing is crucial, traditional marketing methods can still be effective in reaching certain audiences.

Here are some traditional marketing strategies to consider:

- **Print Advertising:**

  Use print advertisements in newspapers, magazines, and industry publications to reach your target audience.

  Ensure your ads are visually appealing and convey a clear message.

  Use graphic design tools like Adobe InDesign, Canva, and CorelDRAW to create your print ads.

- Direct Mail:

Send personalized direct mail pieces to potential and existing customers.

This could include catalogs, brochures, postcards, and promotional offers.

Use direct mail tools like Vistaprint, Postalytics, and Mailchimp to create and manage your direct mail campaigns.

- Television and Radio Advertising:

 Use TV and radio ads to reach a broad audience. Develop compelling ad campaigns that capture attention and communicate your value proposition effectively.

 Use media buying tools like Strata, Mediaocean, and WideOrbit to plan and buy TV and radio ads.

- Outdoor Advertising:

Utilize billboards, transit ads, and other outdoor advertising options to increase brand visibility in high-traffic areas.

Use outdoor advertising tools like Lamar Advertising, Outfront Media, and Clear Channel Outdoor to plan and execute your outdoor ad campaigns.

Personalizing Marketing Efforts

Personalization can significantly enhance the effectiveness of your marketing efforts.

Here are some ways to personalize your marketing:

- Segment Your Audience:

Divide your audience into segments based on demographics, behavior, and preferences.

This allows you to create targeted campaigns that resonate with each segment.

Use audience segmentation tools like HubSpot, Segment, and Klaviyo to segment your audience.

- Use Personalized Content:

Tailor your content to address the specific needs and interests of different audience segments.

Use personalized email campaigns, product recommendations, and targeted ads to increase engagement.

Use personalization tools like Dynamic Yield, Optimizely, and Evergage to personalize your content.

- Leverage Customer Data:

  Use customer data and analytics to gain insights into your audience's preferences and behavior.

  Use this information to create more relevant and personalized marketing messages.

  Use customer data platforms (CDPs) like Salesforce, Adobe Experience Cloud, and Tealium to manage and analyze customer data.

Enhancing Your Brand's Online Presence

A strong online presence is essential for attracting and retaining customers.

Here are some strategies to enhance your brand's online presence:

- Website Optimization:

Ensure your website is user-friendly, mobile-responsive, and optimized for search engines.

Provide clear and easy navigation, fast loading times, and valuable content to enhance the user experience.

Use website optimization tools like Google PageSpeed Insights, GTmetrix, and Hotjar to improve your website.

- Social Media Engagement:

Actively engage with your audience on social media platforms.

Respond to comments, messages, and reviews promptly.

Share valuable content and participate in conversations to build a strong online community. Use social media engagement tools like Hootsuite, Sprout Social, and Mention to manage your social media presence.

- Online Reputation Management:

Monitor your online reputation and address any negative feedback or reviews promptly.

Encourage satisfied customers to leave positive reviews and testimonials.

Use online reputation management tools like Trustpilot, Yotpo, and Birdeye to manage your online reputation.

Implementing Data-Driven Marketing Techniques

Data-driven marketing can help you make informed decisions and optimize your marketing efforts.

Here are some ways to implement data-driven marketing:

- Collect and Analyze Data:

Use analytics tools to collect data on your marketing activities, website traffic, and customer behavior.

Analyze this data to gain insights into what works and what doesn't.

Use analytics tools like Google Analytics, Mixpanel, and Pendo to collect and analyze data.

- **A/B Testing:**

  Conduct A/B testing to compare different versions of your marketing materials, such as emails, landing pages, and ads.

  Use the results to determine which version performs better and make data-driven decisions.

  Use A/B testing tools like Optimizely, VWO, and Unbounce to run A/B tests.

- Predictive Analytics:

Use predictive analytics to forecast future trends and customer behavior.

This can help you identify opportunities and make proactive adjustments to your marketing strategies.

Use predictive analytics tools like IBM Watson, SAS, and RapidMiner to implement predictive analytics.

Boosting Online Sales Channels

Improving E-commerce Platforms

Enhancing your e-commerce platform can significantly boost your online sales.

Here are some strategies to improve your e-commerce platform:

- User Experience (UX) Design:

Ensure your e-commerce site offers a seamless and intuitive user experience.

Simplify navigation, improve site speed, and make the checkout process as straightforward as possible.

Use UX design tools like Adobe XD, Sketch, and Figma to design and optimize your e-commerce site.

- **Product Descriptions and Images:**

 Provide detailed and accurate product descriptions along with high-quality images.

 This helps customers make informed purchasing decisions and reduces the likelihood of returns.

 Use product photography tools like Adobe Lightroom, Canva, and GIMP to enhance your product images.

- **Customer Reviews and Testimonials:**

Display customer reviews and testimonials prominently on your product pages.

Positive reviews build trust and encourage potential customers to make a purchase.

Use review management tools like Trustpilot, Yotpo, and Feefo to collect and display customer reviews.

- Payment Options:

Offer multiple payment options to cater to different customer preferences.

This includes credit/debit cards, digital wallets, and alternative payment methods like Buy Now, Pay Later (BNPL).

Use payment gateway tools like Stripe, PayPal, and Square to manage your payment options.

Utilizing Marketplaces

Selling on popular online marketplaces can help you reach a larger audience and increase sales.

Here are some tips for leveraging marketplaces:

- **Choose the Right Marketplaces:**

 Select marketplaces that align with your target audience and product categories.

 Popular options include Amazon, eBay, Etsy, and Walmart.

 Research each marketplace's audience and policies to determine the best fit for your products.

- Optimize Listings:

Create detailed and optimized product listings with clear descriptions, high-quality images, and relevant keywords.

This helps your products rank higher in search results and attracts more customers.

Use listing optimization tools like Helium 10, Jungle Scout, and Sellics to optimize your listings.

- **Utilize Marketplace Advertising:**

 Invest in advertising options offered by marketplaces to increase visibility and drive sales.

 This includes sponsored product ads, display ads, and promotional campaigns.

 Use marketplace advertising tools like Amazon Advertising, eBay Promoted Listings, and Etsy Ads to manage your advertising campaigns.

- **Manage Inventory and Fulfillment:**

 Ensure you have efficient inventory management and fulfillment processes in place.

 This helps you meet customer demand and maintain high seller ratings.

 Use inventory management tools like TradeGecko, Orderhive, and ShipStation to manage your inventory and fulfillment.

Enhancing Website UX/UI

A well-designed website can significantly impact your online sales.

Here are some strategies to enhance your website's UX/UI:

- Mobile Optimization:

Ensure your website is fully optimized for mobile devices.

This includes responsive design, fast loading times, and easy navigation on smaller screens.

Use mobile optimization tools like Google Mobile-Friendly Test, AMP, and MobileAction to optimize your site for mobile.

- Simplified Navigation:

Organize your website's navigation in a logical and intuitive manner.

Use clear categories, filters, and search functionality to help users find what they're looking for quickly.

Use navigation design tools like Mega Menu, WP Mega Menu, and Menu by Supsystic to improve your site's navigation.

- Clear Calls-to-Action (CTAs):

Use clear and compelling CTAs throughout your website to guide users towards desired actions, such as making a purchase or signing up for a newsletter.

Use CTA optimization tools like OptinMonster, Thrive Leads, and Sumo to create effective CTAs.

- User-Friendly Checkout Process:

Simplify the checkout process by minimizing the number of steps required to complete a purchase.

Offer guest checkout options and provide clear progress indicators.

Use checkout optimization tools like Shopify, WooCommerce, and BigCommerce to enhance your checkout process.

Optimizing for Mobile Sales

With the increasing use of mobile devices for online shopping, optimizing for mobile sales is crucial.

Here are some strategies to consider:

- Mobile-Friendly Design:

Ensure your website and e-commerce platform are fully optimized for mobile devices.

This includes responsive design, easy navigation, and fast loading times.

Use mobile design tools like Sketch, InVision, and Marvel to create mobile-friendly designs.

- Mobile Payment Options:

Offer mobile-friendly payment options, such as digital wallets (Apple Pay, Google Wallet) and one-click checkout solutions.

Use payment gateway tools like Stripe, PayPal, and Square to manage mobile payment options.

- **Mobile Apps:**

 Consider developing a mobile app for your business.

 Apps can provide a more personalized shopping experience and offer additional features, such as push notifications and in-app promotions.

 Use app development tools like Flutter, React Native, and Xamarin to create your mobile app.

- **Mobile Marketing:**

  Utilize mobile marketing strategies, such as SMS marketing, mobile ads, and location-based marketing, to reach and engage with your mobile audience.

  Use mobile marketing tools like Twilio, Leanplum, and Airship to manage your mobile marketing campaigns.

Leveraging Affiliate Marketing and Partnerships

Affiliate marketing and partnerships can help you expand your reach and drive sales.

Here are some strategies to leverage these opportunities:

- **Affiliate Programs:**

  Set up an affiliate program to incentivize individuals and businesses to promote your products.

  Offer attractive commissions and provide affiliates with marketing materials and support.

  Use affiliate marketing tools like ShareASale, CJ Affiliate, and Rakuten Marketing to manage your affiliate program.

- Influencer Collaborations:

Partner with influencers in your industry to promote your products to their followers.

Choose influencers whose audience aligns with your target market.

Use influencer marketing tools like AspireIQ, Upfluence, and Influencity to manage your influencer collaborations.

- **Joint Ventures and Partnerships:**

Form strategic partnerships with other businesses to cross-promote products and services.

This can help you tap into new customer bases and drive mutual growth.

Use partnership management tools like PartnerStack, Crossbeam, and Allbound to manage your joint ventures and partnerships.

Improving Sales Processes and Techniques

Streamlining Sales Processes

Efficient sales processes are crucial for maximizing productivity and closing deals.

Here are some ways to streamline your sales processes:

- Sales Pipeline Management:

Use a CRM system to manage your sales pipeline and track leads throughout the sales cycle.

This helps you prioritize high-potential leads and ensure timely follow-ups.

Use CRM tools like Salesforce, HubSpot, and Zoho CRM to manage your sales pipeline.

- Automate Repetitive Tasks:

Automate repetitive tasks, such as data entry, lead nurturing, and follow-up emails, to free up your sales team's time for more strategic activities.

Use automation tools like Zapier, Automate.io, and IFTTT to automate tasks.

- **Standardize Sales Procedures:**

  Develop standardized sales procedures and best practices to ensure consistency and efficiency.

  Provide training and resources to your sales team to ensure they adhere to these standards.

  Use documentation tools like Confluence, Notion, and Google Docs to create and share sales procedures.

- **Continuous Improvement:**

  Regularly review and analyze your sales processes to identify areas for improvement.

  Implement changes based on feedback and performance metrics.

  Use performance tracking tools like SalesLoft, Outreach, and Gong.io to monitor and improve sales processes.

Training and Empowering Your Sales Team

A well-trained and motivated sales team is essential for driving sales growth.

Here are some strategies to train and empower your sales team:

- **Sales Training Programs:**

 Implement comprehensive sales training programs that cover essential skills, such as prospecting, closing techniques, and objection handling.

 Provide ongoing training to keep your team updated with the latest trends and best practices.

 Use training platforms like Lessonly, Brainshark, and LinkedIn Learning to deliver sales training.

- **Coaching and Mentoring:**

  Pair less experienced sales reps with seasoned mentors who can provide guidance and support.

  Regular coaching sessions can help your team refine their skills and stay motivated.

  Use coaching tools like Chorus.ai, ExecVision, and LevelEleven to manage coaching and mentoring programs.

- **Empowerment and Autonomy:**

Empower your sales team by giving them the autonomy to make decisions and take ownership of their performance.

Encourage a culture of accountability and continuous improvement.

Use performance management tools like Betterworks, 15Five, and Lattice to support empowerment and autonomy.

- Incentives and Recognition:

Offer attractive incentives and recognition programs to motivate your sales team.

This could include performance-based bonuses, sales contests, and public recognition for outstanding achievements.

Use incentive management tools like Xactly, Spiff, and Hoopla to manage incentives and recognition programs.

Using CRM Tools Effectively

Customer Relationship Management (CRM) tools are essential for managing customer interactions and improving sales processes.

Here are some ways to use CRM tools effectively:

- **Centralized Data Management:**

 Use your CRM system to centralize customer data and ensure all relevant information is easily accessible.

 This helps your sales team have a complete view of each customer and personalize their approach.

 Use CRM tools like Salesforce, HubSpot, and Zoho CRM to manage customer data.

- **Lead Scoring and Prioritization:**

  Implement lead scoring to prioritize high-potential leads.

  Use criteria such as engagement level, purchase history, and demographic information to score and rank leads.

  Use lead scoring tools like LeadSquared, Marketo, and Pardot to implement lead scoring.

- **Automated Workflows:**

  Set up automated workflows to streamline sales processes, such as lead nurturing, follow-ups, and task assignments.

  This ensures timely and consistent communication with leads and customers.

  Use workflow automation tools like Zapier, Automate.io, and Integromat to automate workflows.

- Analytics and Reporting:

Use CRM analytics and reporting features to track sales performance, identify trends, and make data-driven decisions.

Regularly review your CRM reports to monitor progress and adjust strategies as needed.

Use analytics tools like Tableau, Power BI, and Domo to analyze CRM data.

Implementing Effective Sales Techniques

Using effective sales techniques can significantly improve your conversion rates and boost sales.

Here are some techniques to consider:

- Consultative Selling:

Adopt a consultative selling approach, where your sales team acts as advisors and focuses on understanding the customer's needs and providing tailored solutions.

This builds trust and fosters long-term relationships. Use consultative selling training programs and tools to implement this approach.

- Upselling and Cross-Selling:

Train your sales team to identify opportunities for upselling (selling a higher-end product) and cross-selling (selling complementary products).

This can increase the average order value and boost overall sales.

Use upselling and cross-selling tools like Pipedrive, ActiveCampaign, and Salesforce to implement these techniques.

- **Solution Selling:**

  Focus on selling solutions rather than products.

  Highlight how your products or services can solve the customer's specific problems and deliver value.

  Use solution selling frameworks and tools to support this approach.

- **Handling Objections:**

  Equip your sales team with strategies to handle objections effectively.

  This includes active listening, empathizing with the customer's concerns, and providing clear and compelling responses.

  Use objection handling training programs and tools to enhance these skills.

Building a Customer-Focused Sales Approach

A customer-focused sales approach prioritizes the needs and preferences of your customers.

Here are some ways to build a customer-focused sales approach:

- Understand Customer Needs:

Invest time in understanding the needs, pain points, and goals of your customers.

Use this information to tailor your sales pitch and demonstrate how your products or services can meet their needs.

Use customer research tools like Qualtrics, SurveyMonkey, and Typeform to gather insights.

- **Build Relationships:**

 Focus on building long-term relationships with your customers rather than just closing a sale.

 This involves regular communication, providing value, and being responsive to their needs.

 Use relationship management tools like Salesforce, HubSpot, and Zoho CRM to manage customer relationships.

- Provide Exceptional Service:

 Ensure your sales team provides exceptional service at every touchpoint.

 This includes being knowledgeable, courteous, and proactive in addressing customer concerns.

 Use customer service tools like Zendesk, Freshdesk, and Help Scout to support exceptional service.

- Follow Up and Stay Engaged:

Regularly follow up with your customers after a sale to ensure satisfaction and address any issues.

Stay engaged with your customers through regular communication and personalized offers.

Use follow-up and engagement tools like Mailchimp, Constant Contact, and Sendinblue to manage customer follow-up and engagement.

Leveraging Technology and Automation

Implementing AI and Machine Learning in Sales

Artificial Intelligence (AI) and Machine Learning (ML) can revolutionize your sales processes.

Here are some ways to implement AI and ML in sales:

- Sales Forecasting:

Use AI-powered tools to analyze historical data and predict future sales trends.

This helps you make informed decisions and plan your sales strategies more effectively.

Use AI sales forecasting tools like Salesforce Einstein, InsideSales, and Aviso to implement AI-driven sales forecasting.

- Lead Scoring:

Implement AI algorithms to score and prioritize leads based on their likelihood to convert.

This allows your sales team to focus on high-potential leads and improve conversion rates.

Use AI lead scoring tools like Infer, Lattice Engines, and MadKudu to implement AI-driven lead scoring.

- **Personalized Recommendations:**

 Use AI to analyze customer behavior and preferences, and provide personalized product recommendations.

 This enhances the customer experience and increases sales. Use AI recommendation engines like Dynamic Yield, Algolia, and Nosto to implement personalized recommendations.

- **Chatbots and Virtual Assistants:**

Deploy AI-powered chatbots and virtual assistants to handle routine customer inquiries, provide support, and qualify leads.

This frees up your sales team to focus on more complex tasks.

Use chatbot and virtual assistant tools like Drift, Intercom, and Chatfuel to implement AI-driven customer support.

Using Automation Tools for Marketing and Sales

Automation tools can streamline your marketing and sales processes, saving time and improving efficiency.

Here are some ways to use automation tools:

- **Email Marketing Automation:**

 Use email marketing automation platforms to send targeted and personalized email campaigns.

 Automate workflows such as welcome emails, follow-ups, and re-engagement campaigns.

 Use email automation tools like Mailchimp, HubSpot, and ActiveCampaign to implement email marketing automation.

- Lead Nurturing:

Implement automated lead nurturing workflows to engage and nurture leads throughout the sales funnel.

This includes sending relevant content, follow-up emails, and personalized offers.

Use lead nurturing tools like Marketo, Pardot, and Eloqua to implement automated lead nurturing.

- Social Media Automation:

Use social media automation tools to schedule and manage your social media posts.

This ensures consistent posting and allows you to focus on engaging with your audience.

Use social media automation tools like Hootsuite, Buffer, and Sprout Social to implement social media automation.

- **Sales Task Automation:**

 Automate routine sales tasks, such as data entry, follow-up reminders, and lead assignments.

 This increases productivity and allows your sales team to focus on high-value activities.

 Use sales task automation tools like Salesforce, HubSpot, and Pipedrive to implement sales task automation.

Adopting New Technologies to Streamline Operations

Adopting new technologies can help you streamline your operations and improve efficiency.

Here are some technologies to consider:

- Cloud Computing:

Use cloud-based solutions for data storage, collaboration, and business applications.

This provides flexibility, scalability, and reduces IT costs.

Use cloud computing platforms like AWS, Microsoft Azure, and Google Cloud to implement cloud-based solutions.

- Customer Relationship Management (CRM) Systems:

Implement CRM systems to manage customer interactions, track sales activities, and analyze performance.

This helps you build stronger customer relationships and improve sales processes.

Use CRM tools like Salesforce, HubSpot, and Zoho CRM to implement CRM systems.

- **Enterprise Resource Planning (ERP) Systems:**

Use ERP systems to integrate and manage your business processes, including finance, inventory, and supply chain.

This improves visibility, efficiency, and decision-making.

Use ERP tools like SAP, Oracle, and Microsoft Dynamics to implement ERP systems.

- Internet of Things (IoT):

Leverage IoT technology to collect and analyze data from connected devices.

This can help you optimize operations, improve product quality, and enhance the customer experience.

Use IoT platforms like Azure IoT, AWS IoT, and Google Cloud IoT to implement IoT solutions.

Benefits of Data Analytics and Big Data

Data analytics and big data can provide valuable insights to drive your sales growth.

Here are some benefits of using data analytics and big data:

- **Customer Insights:**

 Use data analytics to gain a deeper understanding of your customers' behavior, preferences, and needs.

 This helps you create targeted marketing campaigns and personalized experiences.

 Use data analytics tools like Google Analytics, Mixpanel, and Pendo to gain customer insights.

- Performance Tracking:

Analyze sales data to track the performance of your sales team, products, and marketing efforts.

This allows you to identify areas for improvement and make data-driven decisions.

Use performance tracking tools like Tableau, Power BI, and Domo to track and analyze sales performance.

- **Predictive Analytics:**

 Use predictive analytics to forecast future trends and customer behavior.

 This helps you anticipate market changes and plan your sales strategies more effectively.

 Use predictive analytics tools like IBM Watson, SAS, and RapidMiner to implement predictive analytics.

- **Operational Efficiency:**

Analyze operational data to identify inefficiencies and areas for improvement.

This can help you streamline processes, reduce costs, and improve overall performance.

Use operational analytics tools like Qlik, Looker, and Alteryx to analyze and optimize operations.

Expanding into New Markets

Identifying Potential New Markets

Expanding into new markets can provide significant growth opportunities.

Here are some steps to identify potential new markets:

- Market Research:

Conduct thorough market research to identify regions or segments with high growth potential.

Analyze factors such as market size, demand, competition, and economic conditions.

Use market research tools like Nielsen, Euromonitor, and Statista to gather market data.

- **Customer Analysis:**

  Identify customer segments in new markets that align with your target audience.

  Understand their needs, preferences, and purchasing behavior.

  Use customer research tools like Qualtrics, SurveyMonkey, and Typeform to gather insights.

- **Competitive Analysis:**

 Assess the competitive landscape in new markets.

 Identify key competitors, their market share, and their strengths and weaknesses.

 Use competitive analysis tools like SimilarWeb, SEMrush, and Ahrefs to analyze competitors.

- Regulatory Considerations:

Understand the regulatory environment in new markets, including trade regulations, import/export restrictions, and compliance requirements.

Work with legal experts to navigate regulatory complexities.

Strategies for Market Entry

Entering a new market requires a well-planned strategy.

Here are some strategies for market entry:

- Direct Exporting:

Sell your products directly to customers in new markets through e-commerce platforms, international shipping, or direct sales channels.

Use cross-border e-commerce platforms like Alibaba, Amazon Global Selling, and eBay to reach international customers.

- Local Partnerships:

Form partnerships with local businesses or distributors to gain access to new markets.

This can help you navigate local regulations, cultural differences, and customer preferences.

Use partnership management tools like PartnerStack, Crossbeam, and Allbound to manage local partnerships.

- Franchising and Licensing:

Expand your business through franchising or licensing agreements.

This allows you to leverage local expertise and resources while maintaining control over your brand.

Use franchising tools like FranConnect, FranchiseSoft, and Naranga to manage franchising agreements.

- **Joint Ventures:**

  Enter new markets through joint ventures with local companies.

  This provides access to local knowledge, resources, and networks, reducing the risks associated with market entry.

  Use joint venture management tools like JIRA, Asana, and Trello to manage joint venture projects.

Localizing Your Approach for Different Regions

Localizing your approach is essential for success in new markets.

Here are some strategies to consider:

- Cultural Adaptation:

Adapt your products, marketing messages, and customer service to align with local cultural norms and preferences.

This enhances customer acceptance and builds trust.

Use cultural adaptation tools like Hofstede Insights, CultureWizard, and GlobeSmart to understand cultural differences.

- **Language Translation:**

 Ensure your marketing materials, website, and customer support are available in the local language.

 This improves communication and customer experience.

 Use translation tools like Google Translate, SDL Trados, and Transifex to translate your content.

- **Pricing Strategies:**

 Adjust your pricing strategies to reflect local market conditions, purchasing power, and competitive landscape.

 This ensures your products are competitively priced and accessible to local customers.

 Use pricing tools like Pricefx, PROS, and Vendavo to manage pricing strategies.

- Local Marketing Channels:

Utilize local marketing channels, such as regional media, social platforms, and influencers, to reach your target audience effectively.

Use local marketing tools like Yext, MomentFeed, and Synup to manage local marketing campaigns.

Overcoming Challenges in New Market Expansion

Expanding into new markets comes with its own set of challenges.

Here are some strategies to overcome these challenges:

- Regulatory Compliance:

Ensure compliance with local regulations, including trade laws, product standards, and tax requirements.

Work with legal experts to navigate regulatory complexities.

Use compliance tools like ComplianceQuest, MetricStream, and LogicGate to manage regulatory compliance.

- Supply Chain Management:

Establish a reliable supply chain to ensure timely delivery of products to new markets.

This may involve partnering with local logistics providers or setting up regional distribution centers.

Use supply chain management tools like SAP Ariba, Oracle SCM, and Kinaxis to manage supply chains.

- Risk Management:

Identify potential risks associated with market entry, such as political instability, currency fluctuations, and cultural differences.

Develop contingency plans to mitigate these risks. Use risk management tools like RiskWatch, Resolver, and LogicManager to manage risks.

- Local Talent Acquisition:

Hire local talent to gain insights into the market and build relationships with local stakeholders.

Local employees can provide valuable knowledge and help you navigate cultural nuances.

Use talent acquisition tools like LinkedIn Talent Solutions, Lever, and Greenhouse to hire local talent.

Building Strategic Partnerships and Alliances

Identifying Potential Partners

Strategic partnerships and alliances can drive significant growth.

Here are some steps to identify potential partners:

- Complementary Businesses:

Look for businesses that offer complementary products or services.

This can create synergies and provide a more comprehensive solution to your customers.

Use business matching platforms like Partnerize, Crossbeam, and Alignable to find potential partners.

- Industry Leaders:

Identify industry leaders or innovative startups that can add value to your business.

Partnering with reputable companies can enhance your credibility and market reach.

Use industry analysis tools like Gartner, Forrester, and IDC to identify industry leaders.

- Geographic Expansion:

Consider partnerships with companies that have a strong presence in regions where you want to expand.

This provides access to new markets and local expertise. Use geographic analysis tools like Esri, Google Earth, and MapInfo to identify potential partners in target regions.

- Technology Providers:

Collaborate with technology providers to integrate advanced solutions into your products or services.

This can enhance your offerings and improve operational efficiency.

Use technology scouting tools like TechScout, PreScouter, and Wellspring to find technology providers.

Building Mutually Beneficial Relationships

Successful partnerships are built on mutual benefit and trust.

Here are some strategies to build strong partnerships:

- Clear Objectives:

Define clear objectives and expectations for the partnership.

Ensure both parties understand the goals and benefits of the collaboration.

Use project management tools like Asana, Trello, and Monday.com to set and track partnership objectives.

- **Aligned Values:**

  Partner with companies that share similar values and business philosophies.

  This ensures a harmonious working relationship and alignment in decision-making.

  Use value alignment tools like ValueMatch, CultureIQ, and Perceptyx to assess and align values.

- Open Communication:

 Maintain open and transparent communication with your partners.

 Regularly share updates, feedback, and performance metrics to keep the partnership on track.

 Use communication tools like Slack, Microsoft Teams, and Zoom to facilitate communication.

- Collaborative Approach:

Foster a collaborative approach where both parties contribute their strengths and resources.

Work together to solve challenges and achieve common goals.

Use collaboration tools like Google Workspace, Microsoft 365, and Dropbox to support collaboration.

Leveraging Partnerships for Growth

Strategic partnerships can provide numerous growth opportunities.

Here are some ways to leverage partnerships for growth:

- **Co-Branding and Co-Marketing:**

 Collaborate on co-branded products or joint marketing campaigns.

 This can increase brand visibility and attract new customers.

 Use co-branding and co-marketing tools like Canva, Adobe Spark, and Piktochart to create co-branded content.

- **Shared Resources:**

 Pool resources, such as technology, distribution networks, and expertise, to achieve cost savings and operational efficiencies.

 Use resource management tools like Smartsheet, Wrike, and ClickUp to manage shared resources.

- **Market Access:**

 Use partnerships to gain access to new markets, customer segments, or distribution channels.

 This can accelerate your market entry and growth.

 Use market access tools like Salesforce, HubSpot, and Zoho CRM to manage market access.

- Innovation and R&D:

 Partner with companies to co-develop new products or technologies.

 This can enhance your innovation capabilities and bring new offerings to market faster.

 Use innovation management tools like IdeaScale, Spigit, and Brightidea to manage innovation partnerships.

Case Studies of Successful Partnerships

Examining case studies of successful partnerships can provide valuable insights.

Here are a few examples:

- Nike and Apple:

Nike partnered with Apple to integrate fitness tracking technology into its products.

This collaboration resulted in the successful Nike+ product line, combining Nike's expertise in athletic wear with Apple's technological innovation.

- Starbucks and Spotify:

Starbucks partnered with Spotify to create a unique in-store music experience.

This partnership allowed Starbucks customers to influence the music played in stores and provided Spotify with increased brand exposure.

- Coca-Cola and McDonald's:

Coca-Cola and McDonald's have had a long-standing partnership.

Coca-Cola's exclusive beverage supply to McDonald's restaurants has helped both companies achieve significant market penetration and brand loyalty.

Financial Management and Investment for Growth

Managing Cash Flow for Scalability

Effective cash flow management is crucial for scaling your business.

Here are some strategies to manage cash flow:

- Cash Flow Forecasting:

Develop detailed cash flow forecasts to anticipate future cash needs and identify potential shortfalls.

This allows you to plan ahead and take corrective actions if needed.

Use cash flow forecasting tools like Float, Cashflow, and Pulse to create cash flow forecasts.

- **Expense Management:**

  Monitor and control your expenses to ensure they align with your budget.

  Identify areas where you can reduce costs or improve efficiency.

  Use expense management tools like Expensify, Concur, and Zoho Expense to manage expenses.

- **Accounts Receivable Management:**

Implement effective accounts receivable management practices to ensure timely collection of payments.

Offer incentives for early payments and follow up on overdue accounts.

Use accounts receivable management tools like QuickBooks, FreshBooks, and Xero to manage accounts receivable.

- **Working Capital Optimization:**

Optimize your working capital by managing inventory levels, negotiating favorable payment terms with suppliers, and accelerating cash conversion cycles.

Use working capital management tools like SAP, Oracle, and NetSuite to optimize working capital.

Investing in Growth Opportunities

Investing in growth opportunities can drive significant sales growth.

Here are some areas to consider:

- **Product Development:**

 Invest in research and development (R&D) to create new products or enhance existing ones.

 This can help you stay competitive and meet evolving customer needs.

 Use R&D management tools like LabWare, STARLIMS, and MasterControl to manage product development.

- **Marketing and Sales:**

 Allocate budget for marketing and sales initiatives to increase brand awareness and drive customer acquisition.

 This includes digital marketing, advertising, and sales team expansion.

 Use marketing and sales tools like HubSpot, Marketo, and Pardot to manage marketing and sales initiatives.

- **Technology and Infrastructure:**

  Invest in technology and infrastructure to improve operational efficiency and support scalability.

  This includes software, hardware, and facilities.

  Use technology management tools like ServiceNow, BMC, and SolarWinds to manage technology and infrastructure.

- Talent Acquisition:

Hire skilled professionals to support your growth initiatives.

This includes sales, marketing, product development, and customer service roles.

Use talent acquisition tools like LinkedIn Talent Solutions, Lever, and Greenhouse to hire skilled professionals.

Securing Funding and Financing Options

Securing funding is essential for supporting your growth plans.

Here are some financing options to consider:

- **Bank Loans:**

  Obtain business loans from banks or financial institutions.

  Ensure you have a solid business plan and financial projections to support your loan application.

  Use loan management tools like Kabbage, OnDeck, and Funding Circle to secure business loans.

- **Venture Capital:**

  Seek venture capital funding from investors who specialize in high-growth businesses.

  Be prepared to give up equity in exchange for capital and expertise.

  Use venture capital platforms like Crunchbase, AngelList, and PitchBook to find venture capital investors.

- **Angel Investors:**

Approach angel investors who are willing to invest in early-stage businesses.

Angel investors often provide both funding and mentorship.

Use angel investor networks like Angel Investment Network, Gust, and SeedInvest to find angel investors.

- **Crowdfunding:**

  Use crowdfunding platforms to raise capital from a large number of small investors.

  This can also help you validate your product and build a customer base.

  Use crowdfunding platforms like Kickstarter, Indiegogo, and GoFundMe to raise capital.

- Grants and Subsidies:

Explore government grants and subsidies that support business growth and innovation.

These funding options often come with favorable terms and conditions.

Use grant management tools like GrantWatch, GrantStation, and Instrumentl to find and apply for grants.

Cost Management and Optimization

Effective cost management is essential for maintaining profitability and supporting growth.

Here are some strategies for cost management:

- **Cost Analysis:**

  Conduct regular cost analysis to identify areas where you can reduce expenses or improve efficiency.

  This includes analyzing fixed and variable costs, as well as overhead expenses.

  Use cost analysis tools like SAP, Oracle, and NetSuite to manage cost analysis.

- **Vendor Negotiation:**

  Negotiate favorable terms with your suppliers and vendors.

  This can include discounts, extended payment terms, and bulk purchasing agreements.

  Use vendor management tools like SAP Ariba, Coupa, and GEP to manage vendor negotiations.

- **Outsourcing:**

  Consider outsourcing non-core functions to reduce costs and focus on your core competencies.

  This includes functions such as IT, HR, and accounting.

  Use outsourcing platforms like Upwork, Fiverr, and Toptal to find and hire outsourced professionals.

- Lean Operations:

Implement lean principles to streamline your operations and eliminate waste.

This includes optimizing processes, reducing inventory levels, and improving workflow.

Use lean management tools like LeanKit, Kanbanize, and Trello to implement lean operations.

Monitoring Progress and Adjusting Strategies

Setting Key Performance Indicators (KPIs)

Key performance indicators (KPIs) are essential for measuring the success of your growth strategies.

Here are some KPIs to consider:

- **Sales Revenue:**

 Track your total sales revenue and revenue growth over time.

 This is a direct indicator of your sales performance.

 Use sales analytics tools like Salesforce, HubSpot, and Zoho CRM to track sales revenue.

- **Customer Acquisition Cost (CAC):**

Measure the cost of acquiring new customers.

This includes marketing and sales expenses divided by the number of new customers acquired.

Use CAC calculation tools like HubSpot, Marketo, and Pardot to measure customer acquisition cost.

- Customer Lifetime Value (CLV):

Calculate the total revenue you can expect from a customer over their lifetime.

This helps you understand the long-term value of your customers.

Use CLV calculation tools like Kissmetrics, Woopra, and Baremetrics to measure customer lifetime value.

- Conversion Rate:

 Track the percentage of leads or visitors who convert into customers.

 This helps you assess the effectiveness of your sales and marketing efforts.

 Use conversion rate optimization tools like Optimizely, VWO, and Unbounce to measure and improve conversion rates.

- **Customer Satisfaction:**

  Use customer satisfaction surveys and Net Promoter Scores (NPS) to gauge customer satisfaction and loyalty.

  Use customer satisfaction tools like SurveyMonkey, Qualtrics, and Typeform to measure customer satisfaction.

Regularly Reviewing and Analyzing Performance

Regular performance reviews are essential for staying on track and making informed decisions.

Here are some steps to review and analyze performance:

- **Monthly and Quarterly Reviews:**

 Conduct regular reviews of your KPIs and performance metrics.

 This allows you to identify trends, track progress, and address any issues promptly.

 Use performance review tools like Salesforce, HubSpot, and Zoho CRM to conduct regular reviews.

- **Data Analysis:**

 Use data analytics tools to analyze your performance data.

 Look for patterns, correlations, and insights that can inform your decision-making.

 Use data analysis tools like Google Analytics, Mixpanel, and Pendo to analyze performance data.

- Feedback and Input:

Gather feedback from your sales team, customers, and stakeholders.

Use this feedback to identify areas for improvement and adjust your strategies accordingly.

Use feedback tools like SurveyMonkey, Qualtrics, and Typeform to gather feedback.

- Benchmarking:

Compare your performance against industry benchmarks and competitors.

This helps you understand your relative position and identify opportunities for growth.

Use benchmarking tools like Gartner, Forrester, and IDC to benchmark your performance.

Being Flexible and Adjusting Strategies as Needed

Flexibility is crucial for adapting to changing market conditions and achieving sustained growth.

Here are some strategies for staying flexible:

- Agile Approach:

Adopt an agile approach to your business operations and decision-making.

This involves being responsive to changes, experimenting with new ideas, and iterating quickly.

Use agile management tools like Jira, Asana, and Trello to implement agile practices.

- **Scenario Planning:**

 Develop multiple scenarios and contingency plans to prepare for different market conditions.

 This helps you stay prepared and adapt to unexpected changes.

 Use scenario planning tools like SAP, Oracle, and NetSuite to develop and manage scenarios.

- **Continuous Learning:**

  Foster a culture of continuous learning and improvement.

  Encourage your team to stay updated with industry trends, best practices, and new technologies.

  Use learning management tools like LinkedIn Learning, Udemy, and Coursera to support continuous learning.

- **Customer Feedback Loop:**

  Maintain an ongoing feedback loop with your customers.

  Use their input to refine your products, services, and strategies.

  Use feedback tools like SurveyMonkey, Qualtrics, and Typeform to gather and analyze customer feedback.

Conclusion

Recap of Key Strategies

Achieving significant sales growth requires a comprehensive and multifaceted approach.

Throughout this guide, we've covered various strategies to help you add another zero to your business sales in 2024-25.

These suggestions include conducting thorough market research, enhancing product offerings, optimizing sales and marketing efforts, leveraging technology, expanding into new markets, building strategic partnerships, and managing finances effectively.

Encouragement and Motivation for Taking Action

Scaling your business to new heights is an ambitious goal, but with the right strategies and mindset, it is achievable.

Take proactive steps to implement the ideas outlined in this guide, and stay committed to continuous improvement and innovation.

Remember, growth is a journey, and every effort you make brings you closer to your goals.

Final Thoughts on Achieving Exponential Sales Growth

In conclusion, adding another zero to your business sales is a transformative goal that requires dedication, strategic planning, and adaptability.

By focusing on understanding your market, delivering exceptional value to your customers, and leveraging the power of technology and partnerships, you can drive significant sales growth and position your business for long-term success.

Embrace the challenges and opportunities that come your way, and stay motivated on your path to achieving exponential sales growth in 2024-25 and beyond.

Please use the next few pages for your notes and debates.

www.ingramcontent.com/pod-product-compliance
Lightning Source LLC
Chambersburg PA
CBHW071827210526
45479CB00001B/21